Schooling
as you hack

D1077642

Schooling as you hack

Getting your horse fit

By Daniela Bolze

The publishers recommend that all riders should wear correct clothing and a riding hat that meets current safety standards whenever they are riding their horse. When riding on the roads it is important to be aware of local laws regarding horses on the road, to know the local highway code and to wear high-visibility clothing in order to be seen by other road users. If you are in any doubt about your horse's safety on the road always ride with another rider until it is properly trained.

Copyright 2005 by Cadmos Verlag, Brunsbek
Typesetting and design: Ravenstein, Verden
Front cover: Daniela Bolze
Photos: Daniela Bolze, Christiane Slawik
Print: Westermann Druck, Zwickau
Edited by Jaki Bell
Translated by Claire Lilley

Published in Germany

USBB 3-86127-916-2

Contents

1 Where there's a will there's a way

This Fjord mare is only trained for dressage whilst hacking out and really enjoys her work. Please note that is always advisable to wear correct clothing and a riding hat that meets current safety standards. (Photo: Christiane Slawik

Are you one of those people who have forced upon them the importance of school work to improve the flexibility of your horse, but have no arena to use? Then join the club. I personally have been put under pressure for years to ride endlessly school movements such as shoulder-in, leg yield, flexion, bending and collection. Hacking out could be your solution.

There are great excuses for not hacking out: "I only have time for a short hack (which lasts for an hour)." "I am too stressed today." Or alternatively: "My horse is not good outside." Mare owners especially say: "My horse is in season." This is astonishing, bearing in mind that mares have a twelve month menstrual cycle. Or: "The ground is too wet." This is a valid reason, every hill has a risk of being slippery – but not all year round.

Finally, I hate to admit, even I was allowing my horse to go along on his forehand. The relaxing hack was just boring. I knew all the routes by heart and my horse was as wooden as a merry-go-round horse. I could not carry on like this.

It was especially annoying as one can see that the bookshelves are full of a variety of works from the old classical dressage masters to new instructions on horsemanship such as dominance training, or Join-up.

It became clear to me that I was a responsible, horse-loving rider but I was getting nowhere with improving my horse's suppleness and basic training. I felt responsible for allowing him to go around more like a pack horse than a riding horse with a saddle weighing more than 60 kilos.

I began to see dressage in a different light; not as artistic manoeuvres always ridden in the same arena but as a basic standard of training for

Some of the trophies belonging to the Thoroughbred mare, Second Fire who was almost fully trained to advanced level dressage when hacking out.

The Scales of Training

The scales of training are not only for the systematic basic schooling of every horse, regardless of which discipline he is to be used for, but also to give a uniformity to the training system.

Training your horse can be divided into three phases;
- Understanding your horse
- The development of forwardness
- The development of engagement

The phases include;

Suppleness, rhythm, freedom of movement, contact, straightness, balance, working through the back, impulsion and collection. None of the nine principles can work alone but compliment each other and develop side by side. They all work together to achieve 'throughness' or working through the back.

Suppleness means a freedom of movement with a swinging back and supple, loose muscle movement. Submissiveness is not only a mental and physical development, but is the result of working through the back and in a rhythm.

Rhythm means an even length of stride in a regular beat in the three gaits.

Contact is the steady, soft connection between the rider's hands and the horse's mouth. It is sought by the horse and held by the rider.

Impulsion is the transfer of impulsive energy from the hindquarters to the movement of the horse as a whole. It is based upon energy and swing in the moment of elevation propelling the horse forwards.

A horse is then **ridden straight** when the hind quarters and the forehand are in alignment. The tracks of the horse's hind and front feet should line up on both curved and straight lines. As a result of this the horse finds his **balance**.

Collection is the pinnacle of gymnastic basic training. The weight of the horse is divided equally between all four limbs. The hind legs take more weight by strengthening the muscles of the haunches and step further under the body; the horse moves in an uphill direction. Self-carriage of the horse develops through collection.

Submissiveness is the willingness of the horse to obey the rider's aids and respond to them without constraint both mentally and physically.

(More comprehensive explanations of the principles of the Scales of Training can be found in the book, Elements of Training by Kurt Albrecht von Ziegner)

good riding. When working too intensively with the Scales of Training (see opposite) you have no chance to relax and enjoy your horse when riding him.

As a rider who only hacks in her free time and wanting to ride and understand the requirements of gymnastic dressage exercises, I could never find an even, consistently dry riding track. Once, when I was hacking out on good going in the countryside, I had the idea that it was the ideal training area for all dressage exercises: grass verges for shoulder-fore and shoulder-in; lines of trees for serpentines; riding circles around single trees on level ground and spiralling in and out; going up and down hill for collected work; muddy areas for shortening the trot strides, and so on. I had to learn to be creative to use what I could for my purpose. I would like this book to be your guide to being creative for yourself to bring more fun and quality into your everyday riding.

Secondly, I would like to give you great exercises when riding in a group. Riding just in a single line with horses that always go in the same order along the same tracks becomes boring very quickly. It is much more fun when horses are more attentive, more trustworthy and easier to ride.

When in the school …

From a safety angle, a dry school with an even, soft surface that is not too deep gives security to the rider, but I must say that many horses are correctly ridden without ever going into a dressage arena. Work in the school makes accurate riding easier. When you have a riding arena close to you it gives you the possibility to ride your horse on a smooth surface in an even rhythm without worrying about the state of the ground.

With a really nice soft surface the horse will willingly try to take more weight on his hind legs and step under more. It is easier for him to round his back and loosen up. It is similar to us running on various surfaces: hard asphalt causes back ache and joint pain; running in deep sand is tiring and laborious and fallen branches lying in the woods make you anxious about tripping up or falling over. The ideal situation for running sports is a purpose built running track with a light, soft ash surface and a proper foundation.

You at least need an area with minimum distractions to give your horse a chance to concentrate. Above all, it is important to have lessons to improve your skills as a rider and the training level of your horse with a riding instructor in the riding school. Standing in the middle of the school the instructor can see all his or her pupils and keep them under control. On your own when you are hacking out without your instructor present you must concentrate on your own horse.

I find it a good policy to occasionally give lessons to horse and rider while hacking. This is also a test for

A reliable even surface gives a young horse the security to step under himself and remain straight

the professional – is he only good at the theory or can he put his know-how into practice in an outdoor situation? In negative situations does he know what to do without hesitation, as a good riding instructor would? For a short period of time you can ride side by side with the horses at a safe distance apart.

Always riding on the same surface with no unforeseen circumstances allows riders a greater control over their position and correct application of the aids. Each corner is always the same size requiring the same flexion. It is easy for me to perfect my aids in the confines of the school which helps me work together with my horse and enables us to cope with any incidents that may occur when out hacking. When there is room in the school to ride around the track without having to avoid other riders, I can ride my horse accurately on one track keeping

Progressive pole work exercises are best done in the arena or indoor school.

the same flexion, and controlling and correcting the straightness of his body with my legs which is very important to establish, especially with young horses.

Last but not least, cavalletti and pole work is possible in the safety of the school.

The benefits of riding in the arena or indoor school are:

- Ground that remains flat and even enables work in a clear rhythm
- A greater degree of concentration
- An ideal situation for riding lessons
- Control where the aids can clearly be given at the markers

If your horse is keen to argue with you and you need to find a way of restraining him sometimes you will need to ride in the school, to control the exercises and not lose the responsiveness to the aids. Whether schooling or hacking, it is always advisable to wear a riding hat that meets current safety standards.

The biggest danger of pure school-work is boredom. Many horses churn out their training and dressage pro-gramme as a matter of routine – but only when they receive no stimulation from the rider. With input from the rider, there are a number of creative exercises for use in the school.

Horses that are mainly ridden in the indoor school over a long period of time become less sensitive. They become quickly mentally switched-off and in many instances as miserable as animals that are shut in the stable without turnout – afraid and disturbed.

Contact with nature is difficult if they are shut away from outside contact. If you bring such an animal suddenly outside where it smells unfamiliar scents, hears background noise, wind and weather and other animals, the horse who is a flight animal by nature, will panic and he will let his rider know that he does not want to go outside. This crisis must be dealt with by following a quiet horse out on a hack until the habit is broken.

A large dressage arena or indoor school 40 metres by 60 metres limits the movement of a horse. A good long stretch for a quiet canter to allow all the muscles and tendons to stretch and develop is not possible in such an area and in most cases arenas and riding schools are smaller than this and so the horse is always restricted in his movement. When he is properly worked outside the horse is certain to have a good gymnastic work out.

Beside that many riders are on the slippery slope of too much intensive work in the school. They are concentrating so much on the exercises they are riding that they are unaware of other signs from the horse. It so often happens that you come in or out of the school due to frustration. Taking a short hack one day instead and riding a couple of short exercises along a fence would be a much better idea.

... And when hacking?

There is certainly an advantage for gymnastic work when hacking. It is easy to string exercises together. Horse and rider do not fight against each other when riding out. The other main reason is that there is no boredom factor. Even when you ride the same route the seasons are always changing and with variable weather there is always something new: strong wind; a lot of snow; then it's always wet and muddy underfoot or dry, dusty, hard and rutted. Fallen trees or harvest time change the landscape again and again. The whole scene is affected by cars, people, tractors, farm machinery, skateboarders, dogs and so on. The countryside is always changing as it is used.

Horses become more flexible and concentrate much more on the rider's aids when exercising whilst riding out than in the school at the markers. Also when you are making transitions with a young horse and performing specific school figures continually at the same place to give him confidence, the horse actually realises fairly quickly how to react automatically to your aids. With a fresh young horse, and a variety of ground surfaces to ride on, use a steep upward hill for the first canter to help with the brakes. Use uneven tracks for persistent shufflers and horses that stumble or bold horses that tend to storm off, to help the horse learn to concentrate and

Look how easily a serpentine is developed – a wonderful exercise to flex and bend the horse.

to balance on his own four feet, or small fallen branches that the horse has to scramble over. In each instance you must give the horse the correct aids.

In most cases, schooling while you hack is fun for both of you – without losing the effectiveness of training. Enjoying what you do makes regular work easier for the horse when the exercises are later repeated in the school.

The advantages of schooling exercises while you hack

- There is always something new to see due to changes in the surroundings
- There are many ways to build up exercises along the way
- There are variations in ground surface to use for training
- It is more fun – especially in a group
- There is greater mental stimulation

Equipment

2

When you want to ride dressage exercises out hacking the same rules apply to every rider; the equipment you use must fit each horse and also fit the rider, otherwise it can cause pain or restrict movement.

Saddles

It is surprising to see how many horses go around with ill-fitting saddles without it being noticed by their owners, either out of ignorance or by trying to save cost: the saddle can often be more expensive than the horse. Neither situation is good for the horse. You must check how well your saddle fits to your horse's back. A poorly fitting saddle for a horse is just as uncomfortable as you wearing shoes that rub – you would not want to run very far in those!

This means:

Freedom of the shoulder: The saddle should neither lie only on the shoulder blades nor so far behind the withers it touches them with every stride forward.

It must be wide enough in the gullet that there are no depressions left either side of the withers, in the saddle area of the horse's back, after riding.

Freedom of the spine: The saddle panels must be wide enough not to touch the spine so that they do not interfere with movement on curved lines, as happens with many saddles. The panels should both be equally stuffed without lumps in the padding. Such unevenness can appear anyway over a year of use. This can be detected after ridden work, as some parts of the horse's back will be dark and wet, and others dry. Where the saddle patch is dry, it is not touching the back. This can also result from the saddle 'bridging' or not touching the back in the middle which means that there is more pressure on the parts that do touch. With such a saddle we cannot expect good work from the horse. The seat and weight aids will be confusing for the horse and he will misunderstand the meaning of our aids. The freedom of the spine is most important. To make sure of this you should be able to place an upright hand's breadth between the pommel and the withers. Pay attention to the saddle cloth as well as the saddle, making sure it is not tight against the horse's back causing pres-

Here you can see that this rider sits level on her horse. The saddle lies evenly over the back without 'bridging'.

sure. A well-designed, anatomically formed saddle pad will allow air to circulate over the spine. It must be placed forward on the horse's back and slid back into position so the hairs lie flat.

Length of the saddle

For all pony breeds and short-backed horses many saddles are much too long. They put weight on the kidney area that is sensitive to pain and pressure. Pressure on the horse's back causes him to tighten his back when in movement. This does not only result in an unhealthy horse but an uncomfortable rider. Many western saddles are too long in the saddle flaps and tend to lie over the shoulder area, I do not understand why they are designed like this.

A well-fitting western saddle, or an endurance saddle, lends itself just as well to correct dressage exercises as a pure dressage saddle. The freedom of the shoulder movement and the correct length of the saddle are undoubtedly important. No horse can be relaxed when bending if the points of the saddle-tree or the panels are dig-

This endurance saddle fits particularly well at the back but is too close-fitting on the shoulders at the front and could restrict the horse when riding bending exercises.

ging into his shoulder blades or pressing on his kidneys! For riding straight lines a saddle that is too big with wide panels can be used but not when a horse has to bend through the length of his body.

When hacking, you need a shorter stirrup length than when riding dressage in the school. This gives you the advantage of being able to assume a light seat between the exercises in trot and canter for both physical and mental relaxation. Shorter stirrups are better for security and also more comfortable.

☞ **Tip**

Every living being has a good and bad side. Horses are also right and left handed depending on which way they laid in their mother's womb. On the bad side this shows clearly as reluctance to bend in one direction. This you have to work through. If you begin work on the good side, you must repeat the same exercises on the bad side, changing frequently. You must not ignore the problem or give up.

When the horse has self-carriage and understands flexion and bending aids you can ride and train easily with either a snaffle or a double bridle. Please note that is always advisable to wear correct clothing and a riding hat that meets current safety standards. (Photo: Christiane Slawik

of the mouth must be free from pain. The joints on every bit loosen over time and the edges can become sharp, so you need to keep an eye on this. Make sure that the bit is neither too big nor too small. The rings should lay evenly either side of the mouth without pinching when you flatten them backwards. When two or three wrinkles appear on the lips then the bit is the correct height and there is no risk of it banging against the teeth. Before commencing training with your horse, and yearly thereafter, let the vet or dentist check there are no problems with your horse's teeth and especially that there are no wolf teeth present. The bit would press against these and cause the animal pain that he may show by tossing his head about, or by dropping food out of his mouth when he is eating. It is always possible that tension when ridden and some lameness can occur as a result of toothache.

Choosing a bridle entirely depends on what you want to use on your horse. I think it is most important for dressage work that the rider can sit in a good independent seat and can ride with soft hands and not holding tightly onto the reins.

Sometimes when hacking it is necessary to use a stronger bit to produce a better reaction to the aids so that the horse can be controlled quietly and more effectively. There is much more room for the horse to run away should his flight instinct kick in so in these circumstances you may need to control such a horse with a stronger bit.

Some horses react much better to

Bridles

With bits, it goes without saying that they must fit the horse. There is no limit when it comes to comfort and type of bit but the choice is dependent on the horse's stage of training. For example, with a young horse I will only work with either a single or double jointed snaffle.

By using the mildest bit possible the horse learns to move freely forward to the bit. With a straight bar bit the aids are very clear in the horse's mouth and the animal cannot pull forward more that we want him to. The edges poll pressure than bit pressure. The amount of poll or bit pressure is governed by having both top and bottom reins on the bit. Some thick-necked horses and ponies prefer a Pelham or a Spanish curb bit that you can use with four reins. Using poll pressure gives the horse a lighter feel, and you will not have so much contact in your hands. Once you have softness you can work with your horse more easily.

Sometimes, quietly try a new bit to put pressure on a different area of the mouth. Some horses become bit-sour for no apparent reason. Simply try another material or style of bit for a change. The outcome can be inspiring. When the horse has learnt to bend and flex then you can ride well in a double bridle or a straight bar bit. Only a hackamore or a Bosal fail as bridles for gymnastic exercises as due to their design you can get no flexion. You must know what you are doing though – when it comes to trying different bits, a little knowledge is a dangerous thing.

For safety reasons the bridle should have a drop noseband so that the horse cannot pull against the rider's aids, but it should not be so tight that it restricts the horse's breathing. You should be able to get two fingers under the noseband. The horse must be able to chew. Make sure the ears have enough room and are not pinched by a brow band that is to short. This can be seen by the horse scratching or sweating a lot in this area, where the sensitive pressure points near the ears receive excessive stimulation.

Equipment for the rider

Always wear a riding hat regardless of how confident you are with your horse or which style you ride in. The oldest and safest horse can sometimes spook and I can personally remember an occasion where wearing a hat was life-saving.

Riding breeches with a full leather seat are very good. They give you a very good feeling through your seat, as they remain smooth against the saddle. There are many washable, synthetic materials in various colours available, but most of them are not better than leather. You just cannot ride dressage in jeans. Using your legs causes the trouser legs to ride up and wrinkle under the knees, and can cause sore spots or bleeding.

I advise you to wear gloves, not to help you hold on more tightly but for the protection of your hands. It can always happen that a horse has an extremely temperamental day and then it is very likely that you return home with your knuckles bleeding as a result of holding them firmly against the saddle (I speak from experience). Besides which leather reins can rub when they become wet from dampness on the horse's neck. With gloves you have a much better grip.

There are occasions when you may need to ride your horse carrying a whip. Using it correctly you can give clear and accurate aids without losing your seat. The same goes for spurs. Both should be used as a means to

When riding on the roads and in the countryside it is always advisable to wear proper riding gear, a hat which meets current safety standards and high visibility clothing to ensure that you can be seen by other road users and rescue teams, in the unfortunate circumstances that it should be necessary.

reinforce the application of your aids. You should not push with a strong seat or give big kicks with your legs when a short tap with the whip from a flick of your wrist would be more effective.

The aids

3

Every correctly executed aid creates energy. Aids must be sharp, fast and clear and work within three times of asking, otherwise a whip aid is necessary. Please do not push with your seat or pull on the reins. An aid should help the horse, not hinder him. Always make sure first of all that you have asked correctly. When you have you will increase the horse's energy or impulsion. If there is repeatedly no reaction, give the horse a short quick whip aid to get the desired effect; not wild strokes of the whip but a short accurate tap, accompanied by verbal encouragement such as: "Hey, listen!" A softly ridden horse is the result of correctly applied aids in the right strength so that the horse understands your wishes and can make a response.

Weight aids always come first closely followed by the legs, and finally the rein aids. Weight aids are a positioning of the rider's weight, when sitting in an upright position, on the desired side of the saddle. The weight is always concentrated on both seat bones, never on just one. It is important that the rider doesn't just collapse at the hip causing weight pressure on the opposite side of the saddle, which was not the intention. If I collapse my left hip there will be more pressure on my right seat bone and my weight will slide to the right.

In classical dressage the horse should learn to step under the rider's weight. If I want to move the horse to the left I have to load my left seat bone so the horse follows my weight aid. Ideally my upper body remains upright in line with the horse and in the middle of the saddle. Simply put more weight on your inside stirrup with your leg pressed down and this will keep your weight on both seat bones. Please do not stiffen your leg and push it away from the horse. The weight aids are needed to ride in every conceivable direction: forwards and backwards, sideways, on circles as well as straight lines and for sideways steps.

Leg aids means the use of the legs from the knees downwards. The

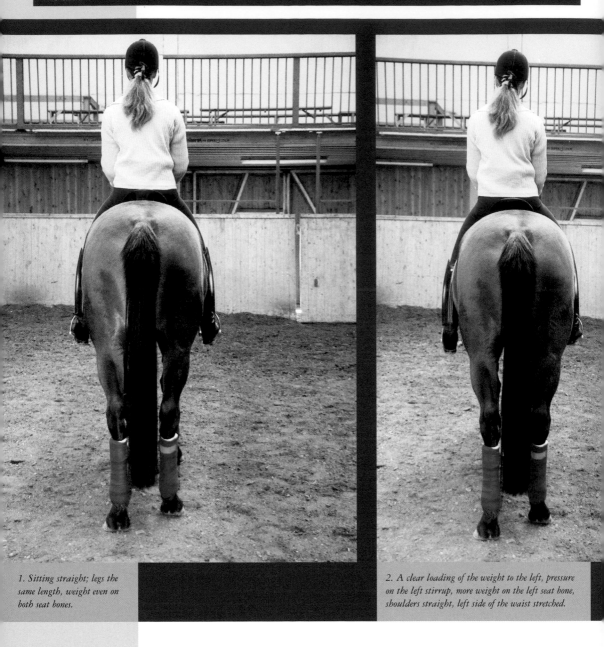

1. Sitting straight; legs the same length, weight even on both seat bones.

2. A clear loading of the weight to the left, pressure on the left stirrup, more weight on the left seat bone, shoulders straight, left side of the waist stretched.

thigh should always be held in place against the saddle without squashing the horse, the rider remaining loose in the hip joints. With exercises on curved lines or circles the inside knee automatically presses a little more than the outside knee. The leg aids are only effective when they are timed at the right moment for the horse to step forwards in response. This goes for stepping sideways as well as forwards.

The legs should not bang around but energise the horse with short

The wrong weight loading with a collapsed [wai]st to the left. The rider's weight drifts to the [lef]t, precisely on the wrong side.

The spurs must be used carefully and precisely so the horse is not pressed with them later than he should have been. He has to have a chance to react. Please do not poke your horse with them! Basic training and sensitising belong in expert hands. In nearly all circumstances in giving an inside leg aid, the outside leg also has a function, at least in a controlling way. It has to be placed correctly to prevent the horse from drifting away to the outside, or it is necessary to support the other leg in forwards driving aids.

The rein aids should ideally be applied with the soft, sensitive hands of the rider. The hand always belongs to the horse, which means that they follow the movement of the horse's head and are not fixed hard in one position. The rider's hands are part of the whole arm up to the shoulder joint. The arm must be carried from a loose shoulder joint, and rest lightly against the rider's upper body with supple elbows, which should be bent and mobile. The rider must be able to maintain a correct position in the saddle without hanging on the reins. This ensures that the horse is not held tightly together by misuse of the reins. Correct rein aids are only possible with the horse working sensitively into the hand in all gaits, without the use of artificial aids, when he is balanced and in self-carriage.

To achieve this, and to take care of your horse's mouth, you need lunge lessons. The rein aids are jointly responsible for direction and the control of the forehand. You should con-

pulses on alternate sides without the knee on the same side rising up. Normally, correct, light backward strokes accompanied by a closing action of the rider's legs are needed to create more impulsion. You can sensitise the horse to your leg aids by using spurs.

This is lovely to see; the hands follow the forehand, the rider's shoulders are parallel with the horse's shoulders and her hips parallel with the horse's hips. The inside leg bends the horse, the outside leg controls the outside leg.

trol the tempo of each gait and execute transitions with half halts so that you can introduce bending and flexing exercises.

The seat aids are the hardest to describe and explain clearly. It is the concept of 'bracing the back' that is often misunderstood. When you just want to sit passively on the horse (which is a nice feeling) you need a loose, but active seat to encourage your horse to go forwards and to improve the way he moves. Furthermore your body must work in a certain way to achieve this. You must sit upright without being stiff. Your spine must follow and absorb the movement of the horse's back all the way up to your neck. You need to use your stomach muscles to support you and not collapse like a wet old sack. The abdominal muscles and the lower back muscles are both needed to give correct back aids. Then by 'bracing the lower back' it is possible to sit with an evenly driving seat and at the same time swing with the movement of the horse's back. The driving power is controlled by your stomach and your pelvis. All of this works in the form of short impulses and not by sustained tension, otherwise both horse and rider become tense. To absorb impulsion and movement the seat must stay loose but with toned muscles; not like a floppy sponge that can be thrown into the air. To follow the strong, swinging motion of the horse's back the rider needs the strength to maintain sufficient controlled movement of the pelvis and back to remain in a good seat at all times without gripping up or collapsing down. The legs control the hind quarters. To drive the horse forward, the seat, whip and impulsive leg aids are necessary. It is important that the horse actively steps under with his hind legs. The horse should naturally always find his centre of balance under the rider's weight. This means that the rider must always keep his weight in the desired direction of movement of the hind legs.

Training while you hack

4

When the ground permits, you could use a field for collecting work. This is the mare, Second Fire.

There are simply no areas of the countryside that cannot be used for training purposes. The safety of the horse is always paramount when choosing somewhere to ride. As a rider, I make sure I am fully aware of the state of the ground. Only when it is safe can I ask for more effort from the horse without him slipping or tripping up.

It is always the rider's responsibility to watch out for the state of the ground. Some horses are wary and very careful about where they put their feet. Such horses will not have the confidence to be ridden in trot or canter when the ground is wet, rutted, hard or stony. Other horses are careless and have no regards for their own safety, which can make then dangerous to ride over difficult terrain.

If the ground is wet you may not be able to ride the exercises completely, and it would be wise to slow down. A lot of mistakes can happen, even in walk. For hacking, winter is often a good time of year for training. The horse's steps must be slow and careful wherever you ride which heightens your awareness of any exercise, regardless of its difficulty.

Training plan

The horse must be both physically and mentally prepared for work whether in the school or out hacking. You need to begin in a quiet walk so that the joint fluid lubricates the joints especially in winter when your horse has been standing for more time in his stable. The horse should have a calm and steady temperament so he is well-behaved and does not spook all the time out hacking. This can be normal behaviour if you do not hack very often, in which case you must be very clear what tempo you wish to ride in so you do not have too fast a ride and use frequent transitions and collected movements to keep your horse's attention. With dressage exercises when you hack, the horse should have a manageable tempo whether he

tends to be reluctant to go forward, or constantly has to be held back. If there is no consistency, it could be that the horse does not trust the rider in which case riding with a companion horse would help him to relax and listen to the rider's aids.

Start with about ten minutes in a quiet but not lazy walk. The horse should be allowed the freedom to stretch his neck as much as he wants. Flex his head slightly left and right to loosen both sides of the neck muscles and to help him flex at the poll. In the loosening phase you can easily change the bend of the neck slightly left and right to straighten the horse. This works best by giving with one hand in a forward and upward direction. These upward movements of the bit in the mouth encourage the horse to soften and in response chew forward and downward. You must immediately encourage him to go forward and then activate the other side of the mouth in the same way.

After the walking phase, let the horse go forward in a free-moving trot allowing him to carry his head long and low. To achieve this keep your hands preferably the height of his shoulder blades and rest them on his neck so that, if the horse lifts his head, he comes against the reins, but the contact is soft if he carries his head in a forward and downward position. The rider should automatically assume a light (forward) seat in the saddle. The hands should remain quiet to give the horse the confidence to step forward to the reins and seek the contact. When in rising trot make

When trotting in the loosening up phase, take the opportunity to flex and loosen the poll.

sure that you change diagonals frequently, as many horses have a preferred diagonal and will put you on their favourite leg which can result in uneven steps. Usually you are told to change your diagonal by sitting in the saddle for a beat, but you can just as easily change it by standing up in the stirrups for one extra step. Standing up in the stirrups has the added ben-

efit of improving your sense of balance. This trot work is important for animals with a lot of energy in order that they can get it out of their system before they can concentrate on work.

When your horse has stretched forward and down to the bit a few times and lets you sit fully on him then you can commence individual exercises.

☞ Tip

In your training programme you must consider the individual temperament of each horse and the weather conditions. Working a tired horse in long periods of trot and canter is not productive work. Transitions in quick succession and frequent changes of tempo make the work more interesting. Temperamental animals tend to overreact at first before they can concentrate fully. They need short spells of collected work in between stretches of trot and canter to quieten them down. On a bitterly cold day change your training plan to include a longer warming-up phase and on a very hot summer's day avoid incredibly long, tiring circular routes ridden at the same tempo.

Even if the horse is capable of going easily into a quiet canter, always loosen up in walk and trot first.

Temperamental horses are often allowed to run away like a train which means that they are in front of the aids and not under the weight of the rider.

After loosening up you should begin with shoulder-fore and shoulder-in. By improving lateral bending it will become easier to ride circles and serpentines around trees. And with an improved contact you can do exercises to ask the horse to take more weight on his hind legs, such as travers, renvers and leg yielding, as well as transitions within the gaits and more advanced collected work.

Grass verges

Grass verges are found alongside all tarmac roads and sand tracks. You can also ride on sand verges and long

All grass verges can be used for most bending and flexing exercises providing the ground is even and not poached.

grass. On the sides of the roads you should watch out for trees that are in your way which you have to go around. This is a good test for the rider's aids. Rubbish or empty bottles are often left on the side of the road so you must always keep your eyes open. When you have a familiar stretch of ground near the stables that you know so well you recognise every stone, you can still come across parts of old bicycles or rubbish and other things to go around on route. Do not use grass verges that are too muddy or chopped up.

Riding straight lines

The hardest exercise for most riders is to see if their horse can stay accurately on a straight line. Even in the school some riders are afraid to let go of their horses and hold them tightly in flexion preventing them from going in a straight line. Hacking can be a helpful alternative.

The narrow lines on the side of the road give you a guideline to ride straight along. They are the simplest of things to use for the most difficult of exercises. Many horses go crookedly in wavy lines, or snack on bushes and trees as they go along.

Use the narrow lines to help your horse stay exactly on the inner track, where possible just using your weight and leg aids. Make sure that you do not use leg aids that are too strong, but use the corresponding leg and seat bone and soften as soon as he goes in the right direction.

So simple, yet so hard – this horse is totally straight whilst hacking, without a wall to help him.

After relaxing for perhaps only one or two seconds you may need to make another correction. In the beginning the horse will probably not stay on a straight line for very long. A few small things will help; sit quietly and be clear with your aids. Use a firmer contact with the right rein if the horse drifts to the left, step into the right stirrup and keep your hips straight and not collapsed. Close both legs around the horse to hold him and look ahead.

Sometimes the horse drifts off the track due to your crookedness, for example a collapsed hip. Correct your own position and sometimes have a friend ride behind you to see how straight you are sitting in the saddle.

Shoulder-fore

Grass verges are fantastic for shoulder-fore exercises. Firstly ride your horse straight on between both legs (with a light contact and correct aids).

In shoulder-fore the horse does not cross his legs. The rider's hips should stay as straight as possible so that the horse is only slightly flexed to the inside through his neck.

The inside leg presses lightly against the horse to drive the inside hind leg forwards, the outside leg stays relaxed behind the girth and prevents the horse from breaking away to the outside. The inside hand moves slightly to the inside without pulling back and the outside hand stays slightly to the outside of the mane and gives as far forward as possible to allow the bend without losing the contact. When the horse's head and neck are taken to the inside in this way (the head must stay vertical as it comes around and not with the muzzle leading so the horse is crooked in the poll) it allows the horse to step through from behind.

☞ **Tip**

With this exercise you can easily discover whether the saddle fits or perhaps you tend to sit to one side, or you sit so extremely to one side so that you are permanently correcting yourself. If the latter is the case then you need to have some with lunge lessons in the school. A crooked rider makes a horse crooked, and vice versa.

☞ **Tip**

The outside aids are extremely important to keep the correct flexion of the horse. The outside rein must stay sensitive and elastic otherwise you prevent the horse stepping through to the contact. The horse must step from your seat and leg aids into the outside rein. With shoulder-fore the shoulders are only slightly moved in, much less than in shoulder-in.

Use a fence or hedge to practice flexion exercises such as shoulder-in, shoulder-fore, renvers and travers.

The inside rein softens on its own instead of pulling the horse around. The horse should be in balance and able to move freely.

The horse should not just be pulled around with the reins but flexed in the direction he is going by using the inside leg and seat bone. The hands are not used alone as a steering aid. The outside rein is more important than the inside rein because it acts as a support so that the horse can take a contact with the bit.

With shoulder-fore the legs of the horse only move in a straight line. Too much bend to the inside would prevent them stepping forwards and cause the front and hind legs to cross. This is why both seat bones should be evenly weighted. In the beginning

just ask for a slight bend to the inside. The horse may not track up, but he will become much lighter in his forehand. Reward the horse for any small amount of improvement he offers. Shoulder-fore as a flexion exercise helps the flexibility of the neck. A free-moving neck is one of the requirements for collection where the weight is taken on the hindquarters.

Here the eel stripe along the horse's back shows very clearly flexion in the head and neck area while the back remains straight ...

... Here you can see the horse bending through his whole back, which is achieved with aids from the rider's seat.

☞ **Tip**

Lateral work should not be ridden in a hackamore. The horse can only flex at the poll and cannot understand the rein aids as they are not precise enough.

Shoulder-in

Shoulder-in is the first exercise for flexing and bending the horse. The amount of bend is only slight and the horse is bent away from the direction of movement. The aids are the same, but you turn your shoulders so they remain parallel to the horse's shoulders. Make sure that your weight is on your inside seat bone and that your inside leg is used to bend the horse through his whole back so that he can go forwards using both sides of his body evenly. When he starts to soften in his mouth and chew the bit it is pressure from the inside leg and the

weight aid from the inside seat bone that ask the horse to bend, and not the reins.

In shoulder-in the horse should cross his front legs and work on three or four tracks, with his hind legs staying on the track. The outside leg is placed behind the girth to prevent the hindquarters swinging away to the outside. This is a good exercise to ride along the lines by the side of the road with or without a hedge as a guide.

Some horses fall to the inside of the track or verge. When the horse tries to do this it is a good idea to use more inside leg and change the weight

Shoulder-in on four tracks, which is more difficult than shoulder-in on three tracks, gives the horse a total gymnastic workout.

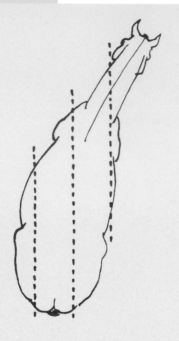

Shoulder-in ridden on three ...

And on four tracks

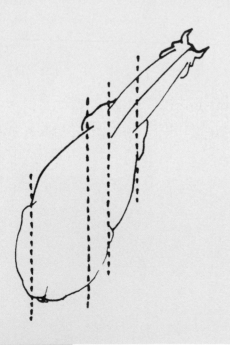

briefly to the outside seat bone as a correction. If this does not work, it is preferable to ride the horse in a small circle, or volte, so nothing else happens by mistake. Let him go straight along the lines and then try the exercise again. This is the best way in the long term.

Transitions

All straight paths are excellent – regardless of how narrow they are – for transitions from one gait to another, from fast to slow, or vice versa. When grass verges are too poached to use for bending exercises it can still be helpful to use narrow ruts when riding transitions to halt as they prevent the hind quarters swinging to one side and help the horse remain straight. They are also useful when riding rein-back.

Riding along tracks

Serpentines

When you have an even tarmac road or sand track to ride on you can easily use it to ride serpentines.

It need not be more than 4 metres wide for this purpose. It is important that the serpentine is ridden with weight and leg aids so that the horse bends properly around the inside leg and does not just do a zigzag from one side to the other.

Only ride serpentine, or any of these exercises, on a public highway if you have full visibility and can see that no vehicles are approaching.

Riding serpentines requires the same aids as shoulder-in only the outside leg presses more firmly against the horse (Sometimes quite a strong aid is necessary!) so that he moves forwards in the direction of the bend. It is also important that the horse is straightened briefly before bending him in the new direction. Sit correctly so that your aids are precise and clear. Your reactions should not be too slow. It is preferable to progress correctly in small stages so that you end up with a supple horse that listens to your aids.

You can also use such tracks to ride leg yielding when the horse has already learnt with the help of a hedge as a barrier. (See the paragraph on fences.)

It is important to know the phases of a serpentine: the first horse is ridden straight before changing direction and the one behind is in the bending phase.

Bending exercises on straight roads and tracks are always useful especially when your horse is too fast and not collected when ridden on open land. You need to ride controlled work in small phases in order that you can not only regulate the tempo of the horse but also control the position of the head and train the right muscles.

☞ **Tip**

A hack should always be a combination of free, forward work (preferably on a long rein, with the weight on the hind legs) and bending and collecting exercises. Between short periods of work always leave the horse in peace. This often needs to be for as long as 100 metres.

This Fjord mare is in a slight travers position. The croup is bent more than the shoulders.

Travers and Renvers

When the horse can be ridden in shoulder-in and leg yielding I use tracks to ride a few steps of travers and renvers. The difference between these movements is whether the head or the croup is towards the wall (in travers it is the head, and in renvers the croup). This does not mean that I can only ride these exercises in the school. When hacking, it is rare to find the right place to perform them, so I have to rely on bending and flexion and improving the strength of the forwards-sideways movement of the horse.

The horse is bent in the direction of movement. Weight is taken on the inside seat bone: for example if you are riding travers to the right you need to sit on the right seat bone. The horse is again flexed to the inside with a softly feeling inside rein, and the outside rein holds the contact. It is the aid from the outside leg behind the girth that bends the croup of the horse around the inside leg. More weight is

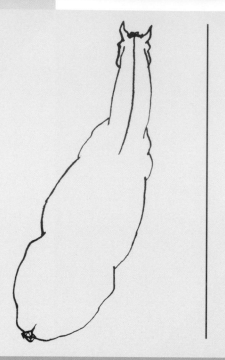

In travers the head is towards a wall, imaginary or otherwise. Flexion and bending is in the direction of movement.

In renvers the croup is towards the wall or side of the school.

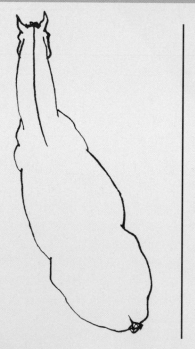

put into the right stirrup to strengthen the weight aid so the horse can step under the new centre of gravity. Watch out: do not tense up your leg otherwise your horse will lean against it instead of bending around it! The rider must make sure that he does not collapse at the hip putting his weight in the wrong place. Also the horse should not be behind the leg causing the centre of gravity to change. Again, the inside leg bends the horse but the rider's outside leg behind the girth asks the horse's outside leg to step under. In renvers the forwards driving power is determined by the position of the horse's hips.

Half Pass

The difference between this and travers is the line along which it is ridden. It is a clear forwards-sideways movement. In half pass there is a danger that the horse will lose the tempo and impulsion or that the centre of gravity will move forward, putting the horse on his forehand. This is why you should not ask for too much all at once otherwise you might unbalance him. It is better to ride just a few steps to get more bending of the joints and swinging through the back. To achieve the forwards-sideways movement, the inside leg has the additional function of asking the horse to go forwards, whereas the outside leg behind the girth is responsible for asking the hind legs to step under and sideways.

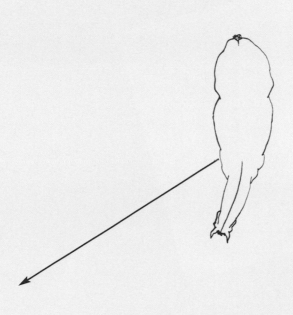

In half pass the horse is bent in the same way as in travers but he moves forwards as well as sideways

Half pass in walk. The rider is less likely to lose impulsion than when riding it in trot.

Choose trees that are not so close together that the horse cannot go around them. The better the training is, the smaller the space can be.

Trees and other obstacles in a row

For serpentines you could easily use rows of trees, fence posts, a line of stones, or other such things for all young horses. You must know the ground where you want to perform your loops and also the obstacles you will be using. It is up to the rider to find a suitable row of trees to ride ser- pentines through as an alternative to riding then along a straight road. Rows of trees demand correct aids otherwise you can very quickly hurt your knees if your aids are not clear. The gaps in the trees must be wide enough for the horse and the rider's legs to go between. It pays to ride a horse that thinks for himself and is able to judge distances independent- ly from our aids.

Sometimes small bushes are better for the first bending exercises than rows of trees. They are also kinder on the rider's knees!

When you begin riding around trees select ones that are not too close together making the exercise too difficult for the horse. At a later stage, vary exercises around the obstacles by riding one or two loops in the reverse direction. For loops, which require the same flexion as for voltes and circles, give the same aids as shoulder-in except that the horse is ridden forwards instead of sideways. Flex the horse so his head is on the line you are riding and you can move his shoulders into the required position. The hands automatically go with the horse. The inside seat bone takes more weight and the inside leg asks the horse to bend. The outside leg controls the hind quarters keeping them on the line of the loop. The horse should always be ridden from the inside leg to the outside rein.

If the horse drifts to the inside or falls onto his inside shoulder, or out over his outside shoulder, do not change your correct seat. Sometimes it feels as difficult as trying to make a drop of water go where you want it to, especially when riding young horses. Staying in the correct seat take your horse back onto the line of the curve or circle, using your outside rein when he drifts to the inside and your inside rein when he drifts to the outside. Support the bend with the inside leg. Trust and time are everything – just believe it will work.

With further training you can ride serpentines on long reins. This helps to develop lightness and willingness to respond to the aids. At a later stage you can ride them in trot and canter on a contact.

> ### ☞ Tip
>
> Ideally the horse steps on curved lines with his hind legs following the track of the front legs. This is described as straightness. The hind feet should step forward over the hoof prints of the front feet, staying on the same line.

Voltes and circles

Single trees give you and your horse a focal point around which to ride voltes (small circles of 6–8 metres in diameter) and circles. The horse should be positioned in the same way as before, by the angle of the rider's shoulders and use of the weight aids. Try making the circles smaller and bigger, as you circle around the tree or stone, by putting more weight in the outside stirrup (to make the circle bigger), or into the inside stirrup (to make the circle smaller). This is a good exercise to improve the use of the weight aids. Support the bend with the outside leg whether moving inwards or outwards. It must be stronger when making the circle smaller than when making it bigger.

Tracking up

No bush or tree is remarkable enough to make a horse track up! As you make your circles smaller, flex the horse with the reins so that his head is facing the obstacle and how much he is able to go forward is limited. Thus he develops impulsion from the hind legs as they cross over. This is actually a turn around the forehand, but be careful that the horse does not just bend his neck or become crooked in the poll!

When hacking, the hardest thing to do is to find a good place to ride circles. You need a large flat, non-slippery surface at your disposal. The circle needs a diameter of at least 20 metres so you need to find a big enough field or area to ride in. If you ride in a field without permission, you will be in trouble. Circle exercises are best ridden in the autumn if you are

allowed to ride on stubble fields, but do ask first! Circles in an open field enable you to ride your horse correctly through his back, in balance and properly in collection where he has no walls to lean on for support. Most horses either drift outwards or fall onto the inside shoulder. You have the ideal opportunity to repeat the exercises, beginning in walk, then in trot, and at a later stage in canter. If you are allowed to ride on a stubble field,

You can see straight away that the rider is behind the centre of gravity as the horse steps across, but she is sitting exactly over the hind leg that is stepping under. Her outside leg is too far away from the horse – a common fault. It is always advisable to wear a riding hat that meets current safety standards when schooling or hacking your horse.

it is a perfect area (like a large playground) to practice flying changes, for example, but choose the best ground to ride on!

Fences

Every hedge, every row of trees, every corner of a field, every fence gives a barrier to ride exercises along when a horse needs support on the outside. A long stretch of ground is common, but rarely is a fence more than 100 metres in length. Riders concentrate on riding exercises again and again along the wall of the school. The exercises are ridden just as well alongside hedges or fences and it is more relaxing. At each hedge, try the exercise again. The ambitious rider will take advantage of all the possibilities that arise when hacking, being aware that horses work better when they have short rests in between the exercises. Be careful when riding along fences that the ground is even and not slippery then the horse can be sure-footed.

Leg yielding

Wooden posts alongside tracks, hedges, fences and every form of natural barrier are useful for leg yielding. Ride the horse straight alongside the barrier. Put your weight in the desired direction, in this example sitting to the left (without collapsing at the hip).

Bring the left rein slightly away from the neck, leading the horse in

If the farmer allows, silage bales are great focal points to ride circles and voltes around

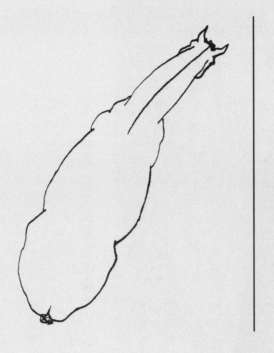

In leg yielding the horse learns to move sideways away from the rider's leg. He is bent away from the direction of movement

the direction of movement, and rest the right rein against the neck. The horse is bent towards the fence. Put the right leg slightly back. When the horse responds to your weight aid and puts his weight to the left use your left leg to ask the left hind leg to step under. Make sure the horse moves over step by step and does not just slide sideways. After a few steps have been successful, try in the other direction.

Many riders forget to concentrate on their position and allow the upper body to fall forwards. Sit upright and deep in the saddle. This enables the horse to respond to your weight aids and step under the centre of gravity. Leaning forwards can also cause the horse to step backwards, as this is the aid for him to rein-back; sitting upright prevent this from happening.

When the horse does not try to find his own balance, it is impossible to move the hind legs. You can only ask the horse's legs to move and step under with your legs, not by shoving with your seat!

In the beginning the horse may lean on the reins. Do not forget that you must not pull on the reins, but remain light and ride with feeling. Most

A fence around a field is highly suitable for flexion and bending exercises

important is the sideways movement. The better this works the more emphasis you can put on correct carriage of the head and neck.

> ☞ **Tip**
>
> The legs and whip only work as driving aids when they are given at the right moment, when the horse is lifting the desired leg up. Giving the aid when the leg is carrying weight prevents the horse from responding.

Turns on the forehand

The next time you come across a fence post or fence try a simple turn on the forehand. Flex the horse again with his head towards the obstacle which should be solid enough that the horse in no way gets the idea to jump over it or plough through it. Begin with a half turn on the forehand to the left. To do this, ask the horse to flex slightly to the right, gently using your right rein. The left rein prevents the horse moving forwards (at this moment it is important that the horse does not use the fence as a brake by running into it) and sideways. Sit with your weight to the inside with slightly more pressure on your left seat bone so that the horse does not soften to the left but turns around the

> ☞ **Tip**
>
> Make it easy for your horse to bend by letting him soften in the direction of his hacking companion, his field or his stable, which he will find appealing.

A wall or a corner gives the horse a barrier in front of him when riding turn on the forehand. The horse steps with his hind legs around his forehand, which stays relatively in the same place.

forehand. The right leg is used by the girth to ask the hind legs to move and step across so that the horse stands sideways beside the fence. The outside leg controls the movement of the horse. This exercise should also be ridden step by step. When the half-turn on the forehand is successful, the horse should end up standing beside the fence. Stand the horse about a metre away from the fence and give the above aids. When the horse can perform the movement accurately in the other direction, the exercise has been successful. Also with this exercise you must be careful that you do not lean forwards causing the horse to step backwards. With whole turns on the forehand begin with the fence in front of you so the horse cannot pull forwards. The quicker and more accurately you can react with small aids the better the harmony will be when riding this exercise.

In the turn on the haunches the forehand moves around the hind quarters. The horse is bent in the direction of movement.

Turn on the haunches

In principle the forehand moves around the hind quarters which step around a small circle on the spot. It is easier for the horse if his back end is placed near the fence to prevent him moving backwards. The reins bend the horse in the direction of movement.. Sit quietly and deeply in the saddle so that the horse has a light enough forehand to be able to cross his front legs. Sit on your left seat bone, with your left leg at the girth and your right leg behind. Maintaining a steady rein contact, half halt to prevent the horse walking forward. Turn him with your shoulders and your outside leg behind the girth. This will prevent the outside leg stepping away. Weight should be put into the inside stirrup to help the horse to turn on the spot and should also be used to activate the inside hind leg to keep the rhythm of the walk.

Changes of tempo

One of the most effective exercises for improving working through the back, concentration and suppleness, collection and the self-carriage of the horse is to ride frequent transitions on a straight line. Transitions can be ridden in almost any part of the countryside even if some of them always have muddy areas or are too short to ride very far in a consistent tempo. Transitions can be made from one gait to another, but also within the same gait.

Walk

To bring the horse together from a normal, fairly long outline, work first with your lower back and alternate leg aids to drive the horse forwards, gradually shortening the reins. If given the correct aids he should flex his poll and round his back and begin to chew the bit slightly. Sometimes this is only maintained for a few seconds. On occasions the leg aids have to be stronger and a firmer contact is needed. When riding you must re-evaluate your aids every second. The better the horse is trained the lighter he is in the contact. In a slightly collected walk the length of stride and tempo

☞ **Tip**

To prevent the horse from leaning on your hands, you must first have a firm contact, then you can give half-halts on either side so the horse cannot set against the bit but do not be rough or use light vibrations of the fingers. A serious fault with many bending exercises is that the horse goes on his forehand. If nothing works check that the saddle fits properly or maybe the horse needs the support of a strong contact to help him balance. Only when there is nothing physically wrong and the tack fits properly can a horse work with a light contact and a rounded back.

can be increased by firstly using more muscle tone in the stomach and back, and using the seat bones alternately. This is strenuous work and many horses prefer to run off in trot in which case soft half halts are necessary from the beginning. To start with, an easier exercise is to increase the length of stride in the walk. Change frequently from a powerful walk to a slow one, and then ride more strongly again. Very soon the horse will improve in balance on all four legs and be lighter to your aids. To slow down the walk or to reduce power, use both legs at the same time, and sit up tall. When you have reached the

Sitting in a collected gait, here going sideways, prepares the horse ...

to go forwards willingly into a more powerful trot with an increase in tempo and more impulsion

desired tempo relax again and give new forwards driving aids with your back and legs.

Trot

To increase power in the trot you can take rising trot but you will develop more impulsion than pushing power, for which you need your back aids to activate the hind legs. With rising trot you can easily ride different tempos within the same gait and keep the horse moving forward and upward without him running away. Give the reins enough to allow the nose to go in the direction of the ground then gradually take them up again without reducing the tempo. When sitting in the saddle give the same aids as in the walk. It is essential that you can sit to the movement of the horse's back in the trot otherwise there is a risk that you will become tense in the back and shoulders and hang onto the reins. Before this happens, reduce the tempo of the trot so that you can sit easily to it, or alternatively, go into rising trot.

For many horses it is quite difficult to stay in self-carriage in a faster tempo keeping a light contact with the bit (for example ponies with thick necks), and they become stronger in the hand. To avoid riding with a heavy weight in your hands reduce the tempo and ride another exercise to help the horse take more weight on his hind quarters such as sideways steps, transitions, trotting on from a rein back, and so on.

Canter

Being able to canter in a regular rhythm is a pre-requisite for canter work when you hack.

For many horses open land is a signal to go storming off, which should not be allowed! When you are riding such a horse it is a mistake to let him run along on long tracks becoming long and hollow in the back in the process. To prevent this, ride him in short bursts up hills, or canter just before the end of the track so he does not have room to speed up. Ride with someone who has good control of their horse in canter and is able to hold back should you have difficulties. Some horses have a problem containing their natural flight instinct, so avoid cantering in groups and riding across open fields.

Make sure you canter on good going. In unfamiliar fields, look out

All the exercises in canter should only be ridden on open land when you have full control of your horse in all paces.

for rabbit holes and big stones. When you can control your horse in canter, ride the same exercises as you do in walk and trot. You can repeat the exercises in a light seat to improve looseness encourage more swinging through the back or sit to a more collected canter. Young horses tend to lean on the forehand when straight and can hollow their backs and become heavy in the hand. In this case decide which canter you want before you start.

Changes of tempo in canter have an extremely gymnastic effect on the horse. The canter can vary from the slowest possible collected canter to a long striding extended canter where the horse can really stretch.

Puddles and muddy areas

Avoid deep mud as it can damage the muscles and tendons in your horse's legs but if the conditions are just a little wet and sloshy, make use of these, in walk, preparing the horse with half-halts beforehand. If you are worried about the walk becoming laboured you can trot where there are a few metres of dry ground or, with horses that are working well through the back, ride some canter work, but do make sure your aids are given softly. In the beginning the horse may take the opportunity to stop but in time he should listen to you better. Muddy areas are good places to ask for more obedience. Normally you would ride around holes in the ground but, if you can, find a shallow puddle that is big enough to ride the horse through – but be careful that he does not try to jump it. It is best if the puddle or muddy area is beside a fence or other barrier so it is not easy for the horse to go around the side. Ride the horse forward and leave him alone in front. Encourage him to go in with leg and weight aids. The quicker your reaction is the less harsh you need to be. React in a second if he tries to evade, take hold of the rein on that side and use the corresponding leg for example, if he escapes to the left, use your right rein and left leg. The horse should be ridden forward between hand and leg. Insist that he go forwards otherwise he will go backwards. Your aids (you cannot take a rest through this) show the horse there is only one way out of the situation, which is through the mud. You have to focus totally on controlling the reactions of the horse so he goes in the right direction. It is very important to pat and reward the horse when he does, giving him a tit-bit if you have one.

> ☞ **Tip**
>
> If your horse wears shoes it is better to choose large puddles of water. In thick mud there is a possibility you may lose a shoe, which can be costly!

Many horses like playing about in streams and lakes, but you can use water for gymnastic exercises.

Water obstacles

Be warned that some horses may have kamikaze tendencies and think it necessary to evade such an obstacle by leaping over it. To prevent this happening make sure the hole is too big to jump over.

Many horses are afraid of puddles, streams and lakes. You could choose to have an easy life and always ride around them, but it is better – but not easier – if the horse can learn to control his fear. The best way to tackle this is with a second horse that has no problems with water, that likes to play in lakes, perhaps even swimming, and wades through every puddle. The inclination of a horse to follow another is very strong and he will do things that he would not even consider when alone. Water obstacles must be dealt with calmly, with patience and a strong belief that it is possible. Do not sit in a forward position in case your horse stops. Stay relaxed and encourage your horse to proceed. Reduce the length of time during which you expect him to take a step forwards, not on the same ride but over a period of time. Do not let him step backwards. If he is really afraid, dismount and lead your horse around, and later lead him through the water. Give your horse trust and confidence. With the first step into the water praise him enthusiastically and finish on a good note, preferably giving him a tit-bit. Let him know you are proud of him. Do not use every ditch or stream you encounter but take your time over this training, otherwise your horse could come up with some new ways of avoiding water.

Transitions on straight lines

Every ride out has certain stretches that are always ridden in the same tempo; hills for a mad canter, or bounding along sandy tracks. Horses learn to do the same things in the same place without having to be asked. So make a change today riding your usual canter track in walk or in trot, and the sand track in a continual even tempo. The horse must improve his concentration and not go along on autopilot.

Straight, even tracks are great for a canter but are also useful for collected exercises to help the horse work through his back. Use ground that you know well so that your horse concentrates on the tempo and not on the going. Collect the horse by asking him to go forward from your legs (not by banging them around but by 'nudging'). Ride a short stretch (about 10 to 20 metres) in a slow trot. Try if you can to ride halt from a fluent walk asking only with your seat aids so the horse does not become unbalanced. After four or five steps trot on again using as small an aid as possible.

The horse must react more and more easily and allow you to collect him to a greater degree. It is important during these exercises that you maintain the muscle tone of your body and you ride the horse with your seat and not just your hands.

On difficult tracks have a relaxed trot or canter on long reins or ride a longer walk phase. You should build up the transitions gradually beginning with one or two, but do not ride more than ten without a rest.

When your horse is submissive and is easy to ride through his back in canter, you could use a combination of all three gaits; walk-trot-walk, halt-trot-halt, walk-canter-walk, halt-

Trees and stones can be used as markers to stop by or for transitions. Make sure your horse halts squarely, as shown here.

canter-halt. Make sure you ask for the transitions correctly. your horse moves freely forwards and does not become unbalanced or laboured in his steps.

Accurate riding to markers

To test how long your horse can stay on your aids counting the number of steps is a super exercise. Ride forwards and halt after exactly ten steps, not after nine or twelve. It is not so easy to do. Many horses need half halts after the fifth step so that they eventually halt on the tenth. Many run out of steam by the ninth step. Find out for yourself how this works for you and your horse and try to improve it. With this exercise you can greatly improve the submissiveness of your horse. You might have an impetuous horse that only halts on step ten when you start with half-halts on three, and then only makes it as far as six steps on some occasions, and ten on others. This exercise works very well when ridden in a group where you can ride next to each other.

Rein back

The same exercise works very well for riding rein-back:

Ride a precise number of walk steps to check your accuracy and the clarity of your aids. When you ride rein-back you should begin by making sure that your horse steps back straight and not too fast or crooked. This exercise puts weight on the hind legs better than any other does but it must be properly executed. This is why it is so important that your horse obeys your leg aids and that you can correct him quickly if he swings his haunches one way or the other. Make the exercise easier to ride by using a half-halt, keep your hands in place to prevent the horse stepping forwards, but please do not pull backwards! Close your legs to ask him to step back and sit lightly taking your weight off his back. You must take your upper body slightly forwards to allow him to tuck his pelvis under. The horse learns with this movement that the way forward or sideways is not permitted, and he is only allowed to go backward. Perform this exercise slowly, step by step. At a later stage you can use transitions such as halt, rein-back, trot, as a great gymnastic exercise. I would advise against riding rein-back for more than a horse's length. Two or three steps are usually enough, otherwise the steps can become too hasty making the exercise ineffective and stressful. No one can learn when they are stressed.

Riding up and down hills

There is no better gymnastic work than riding up and down hills. Above

Second Fire moves backwards step by step with her haunches well tucked under her, as it should be done.

You can use any slope or small hill to ride down but do not lean too far back as this can prevent the horse finding his balance. It is always advisable to wear a riding hat that meets current safety standards when riding your horse.

all it improves tempo. Riding uphill in an energetic walk improves condition and builds muscle; demands greater physical effort when ridden in canter and finally it is tremendous fun.

When riding uphill stand in your stirrups and give your hands forward allowing the horse the freedom of his neck. Do not lean too far forwards, but try to find your balance so that

you can use your legs without gripping on.

When riding downhill, again stand slightly in your stirrups, fold at the hips and stick your backside out towards the rear of the saddle. In this way you free up the horse's forehand and give him room to move and he can find his balance. You should just maintain a light contact with the reins to allow the horse to recover should

Riding rein-back on a slight uphill slope is a strenuous exercise for the horse

☞ **Tip**

For young horses or ones that go too fast when they get out in the open use an uphill slope for the first canter. The gradient prevents most horses accelerating. If the ground is even it helps most young animals to stay in a regular tempo and to keep going in a straight line.

he go too fast and stumble. You should always ride downhill in a slow walk and never go down sideways; always keep straight.

Rein-back on uphill slopes

Riding rein-back on an uphill slope is an extremely gymnastic exercise. No other exercise asks the haunches to tuck under so much. This is why it should be ridden step by step, gradually increasing the number of steps so you do not make the horse sour.

Many animals, especially young horses, try to swing to one side. Pre-

vent this with the same aids as those used in muddy areas to keep the horse straight. If he breaks away to the left correct him by using the

It is enjoyable and simple to use small branches and twigs as obstacles when hacking.

right rein and pressure with the left leg. Lighten your seat to give the horse room to bring his hind legs under. To start with one step is enough, but progress at a later stage to six or seven. It is even better if there is a wall to prevent the horse stepping to one side.

Using Obstacles

When hacking there are always fallen trees or branches lying on the ground on or near the track, which make useful natural jumps. The risk of injury is greater the bigger the jump and the muddier the ground. Instead of jumping over tree trunks and branches, I begin by letting the horse step over them, so they should not be too high.

I ride the horse over the middle of a narrow branch, allowing him to step over it. I vary the exercise by asking him to stand straddling it so it lies between his front and back legs for which he should be praised. Then I ask the hind legs to step over it. When there is only a thick tree trunk available, then I just let my horse walk straight over it without stopping. He should step over one leg at a time; left foreleg, halt. Right foreleg, halt. Left hind leg, halt. Right hind leg, halt . (I ask for halt at the moment when the desired leg is placed on the ground so the horse does not go too fast). This is a brilliant exercise for testing the accuracy of your aids!

If there is a long branch that is not too thick I let my horse step sideways along it. I allow the front legs to step over it and then give the aids for leg yield (for details see the section on leg yield along a fence). At first the horse may be confused having a branch laying between his legs and want to dodge the exercise, but if you take it slowly and step by step he should remain calm and stay under control. This exercise works very well when ridden if you lay branches parallel to a fence, flex the horse towards the fence and ask him to go sideways along them with your aids as described earlier.

> ☞ **Tip**
>
> When the horse understands an exercise you can ride it with lighter aids. When I ride such a difficult exercise that I have to apply strong aids (especially rein aids) then this can be counter-productive. The horse will become unwilling and hard in the mouth. Always train your horse intelligently.

It can be good gymnastic work to ride through mixed vegetation so the horse has to watch where he is putting his feet, but you seldom find a safe enough area as there is always a risk of injury from hidden sharp sticks, or other such things that are not visible.

Take car: in varied vegetation or over twigs lying on the ground, you are sometimes better to lead your horse in hand in case he stumbles.

☞ **Tip**

Be careful when riding over tall plants and small bushes with geldings and stallions as they can easily be injured or irritated in the sheath area by protruding twigs or prickly leaves.

Riding in a
group

5

It can also be very pleasant to relax when you hack with the horse is just thinking about going forwards and not about exercises

Most riders enjoy riding in a group as they like being able to talk and feel safer going out in the company of other horses and riders. Riders can, however, be distracted and not be aware of danger, using the horse as a form of transport for a mobile coffee break. (If you only ride like this your horse will never make progress in his schooling). It is perfectly possible to ride in a group riding exercises that help the horses concentrate, become more supple and work through the back.

Riding from the rear of the group to the front: a great exercise that can be ridden in each gait.

With this exercise the horses should be spaced out more to see and understand what is going on.

Changing position

Statements like these are very common: "Goldie must go in the front as she gets upset at the back." Or: "Max can only go at the back as he always runs off at the front." If you always give in to your horse, you will become his slave, and you will have a fight on your hands if you want to ask him to do anything your way. This is why changing position within the group is such a good exercise. Start in slow easy stages and the most difficult horse will eventually be happy going first when the exercise really has worked.

Ride the horses one behind the other in a line on a straight, wide track. Halt the whole group. The last rider should then walk past the group and stop at the front. If the horses will not stand still it is better if the riders dismount and hold the horses in hand. When there is room, and you can ride the gait in a regular tempo, this exercise works well in walk or later in trot. The ride should go slowly in walk before trotting while more able riders can go in a more powerful walk or trot. If this exercise works riding halt-walk-halt, then try walk-trot. When you are absolutely sure the horses are under control try trot-canter, or slower and more forward in canter. A horse cantering up behind a restless ride will spark off the flight instinct. It is up to each individual rider to keep in control. If you ride this exercise too fast and the whole group canters off, you need to start again from the beginning.

It looks so easy, yet it so difficult for all young horses to stand still.

Standing still

Every horse must be able to stand still when hacking; there are many difficult situations that can happen in the blink of an eye. It is important that you can sit quietly without gripping so you do not unwittingly give the horse the signal to run off. If you cannot sit quietly you will make your horse nervous. Count to three and allow your horse to step forward after you have given him the aid. Pat him. Slowly extend the time he stands still. It helps if you have an obedient horse beside you that is good at this exercise.

When your horse is upset make small circles. Shorten one rein a lot and close your knees. Bring the horse's nose around towards one knee, but do not lift your hand too high otherwise the horse could fall over his shoulder. The other rein is left absolutely loose. The animal will finally stop after a few sharp circles. Loosen the reins and pat him. If this happens again the next time, repeat by shortening the rein on

A lot of knowledge and discipline is required to be able to sit quietly next to and between each other for an entire ride in all gaits.

The greatest feeling is to ride across a sunny stubble field in all gaits next to each other – wow!

the other side. This is also effective as an emergency brake to prevent the horse running off but you must do so before he takes a real hold.

Riding next to each other

Some horses take a dislike to their hacking companion and do not like going side by side – use this in your training. The horse does not listen for the rider's aids. Reduce the time the horses are side by side, watching the ears for warning signals. Use your outside rein and inside leg to correct the smallest sign of aggression. A whip on the inside is useful. As soon as both horses go well side by side they should be praised. Riding side by side should be a good experience. You do not need to ride the whole hack close to each other but just a bit longer each time.

When this works well with two horses try with more in a line side by side. It can be a great feeling when five or six horses can go across a stubble field together in a slow canter! Begin in a slow tempo and look out for the slowest horse. If the difference in tempo is too great and one horse is being left behind do not canter for too long. All these exercises make life with your horse better, not worse. Another progression is to ride next to each other with only one hand on the reins. Hold on with one hand and have the reins in the other. It is great fun to ride like this, but the horse must work through its back correct-

When you want to ride variations in tempo the horses need to be similar in their gaits, transition work and able to work through the back.

ly and be fully attentive to the rider's aids. Another good exercise is to ride in a staggered formation, which is easier to accommodate each horse's difference in tempo, but you need a wide track.

Find a partner whose horse has the same length of stride as your horse's and on a straight track, using full and half halts with the aids of your seat, make some changes of tempo in the walk and trot. Go forwards into trot again. After about ten metres walk again (see the section on changes of tempo). This exercise does not work very well with one horse behind the other as some horses are less submissive and take longer to 'brake' and their riders will need to hold back behind the others.

Counting the steps

This exercise has been written about earlier but it also works well in a group. Riding next to each other to start with will encourage the least experienced horse to copy the others. At a later stage this exercise can be ridden one behind the other. Young horses and horses that do not work through the back need a greater number of steps for the exercise to work to allow every rider time to prepare their horse with half halts.

Napping

Almost every horse has the tendency to stick with others and want to cling on to them, which is the natural herd instinct. Only in a herd does the horse have the guarantee of security during

When riding in a staggered formation you have more freedom to accommodate each horse's individual gaits.

its life. This primary instinct is suppressed when under saddle, but when a horse has full trust in his rider's competence, the rider is accepted as a member of the herd and he feels secure again.

For horses that nap, riding in a group is a great way to go for a ride. Stand still as a group. The most confident horse then goes about 20 metres away and halts. The next horse follows, and so on forming another group. The last horse should always be a confident one who will not panic when left on his own.

As a progression, after another practice ride as above, the weakest horse should be ridden from the group first then followed by the others. To test the improvement in control, as a final exercise the horse that naps is ridden away from the group and then back without going any faster.

Next, trot the horse away from the group and walk back. The next step will be to canter away and walk back, but it is very important that you do not canter back towards the others!

With all these exercises you must always ride your horse quietly between hand and leg but on the other hand you have to correct him along the way in a relaxed and calm manner. When changing direction with a half volte, some horses spoil their reputation by simply running back the way they came. If this happens you must not grip on. Using the respective leg aids correctly, so that the horse softens his sides, will encourage him to relax and work softly into the reins.

The napping horse is ridden at the front of the group accompanied by a confident horse.

As a more difficult exercise the new group can be formed out of sight, but so they can still be heard, just beyond a curve in the track.

Riding in a group

When the horses can be ridden separately then you can ride in a group (a minimum of four riders). Every-

When you have a wide enough track to ride on try to ride alone but do not go too far away.

one rides in the same direction with one rider taking the lead and the others following one horse's length apart, being able to do this on open land is certainly an achievement. It is very important that the horses remain quiet to handle to avoid problems. Stop the exercise and start again if things go wrong.

Holding back

The greatest test for a horse that naps is to hold back as the other horses continue at a slow gait. There is a risk that if the others canter away his herd and flight instincts will kick in.

☞ **Tip**

The more nervous you are the more worried you will be in certain situations and this transfers to the horse. You almost have to meditate to achieve a loose seat and relaxed muscles on specific occasions to avoid creating more problems. You cannot ride without being sure of yourself!

Begin in walk. Halt your horse after a few steps while the others ride quietly on. Pat your horse and let him trot slowly on to catch up. Then keep your horse in walk while the others trot slowly. Pat him and let him trot to catch up without letting him panic and canter. When all these exercises work on a long rein, then you could try in canter. Ask the riders to halt if you have a problem stopping. This is very important when you have different horses on the ride, for example when we had an Icelandic pony riding with us who could not stop, but went off in tolt, his natural pace.

Another variation is to wait while others canter up an incline. You should not let all the horses go at once but canter in succession, otherwise the horses could become too excitable. You need good visibility so all the horses can see each other.

The whole group go off into the distance together – this requires a lot of discipline and self control from both horse and rider.

 Tip

If the problem horse becomes too strong in the mouth and hangs on the reins ride a few steps in rein back, being careful he does not take the oportunity to rear, or move him a few steps sideways. Riding a few exercises will get his concentration better than forcing him go straight forwards. Using the whip may cause him to panic and run off in the other direction.

You should always control young horses with half-halts and not let them just follow the others, otherwise they only pay attention to the other horses and not to you. If you find you are quicker than the rest of the group tell your fellow riders when you want to stop.

Generally when riding in a group you must always keep an eye on the least experienced rider. If you have a horse that bolts with you, then do not canter on this ride, but wait until the next time when he is not around. The rider at the rear should

Use the security and calmness of a horse that is used to traffic to help youngsters become accustomed to frightening things such as cars, tractors, herds of cows and so on.

call out to the leader if there is a problem then the leading rider does not have to keep turning around. She does not have eyes in the back of her head! Do not just shout out the name of the leading rider but let her know what is wrong: "Inge, Goldie is going too fast, please slow down!"

Coping with problems

On nearly every hack there are places or situations that frighten the horse causing him to possibly explode. Often it is not the horse that reacts, but the rider. This means that the rider is not self-confident and says: "Oh God, the field with the bull in it, Max will bolt!" The rider tenses up, shortens the reins and tightens the seat.

The reaction of the horse, which was calm before, is: "My rider is telling me something bad is going to happen. I had better run away." The rider alerts the horse that then tenses up. You can guess the rest.

If you want to avoid these situations, you will never leave the stable. You should ride a safe horse to show you that there are no sabre-toothed tigers out there! Try to radiate calmness and be self confident. Ignore the frightening things and beware of the signals you are giving to the horse. Positive thoughts help such as: "Look, that is all it is. I have already seen it and you do not have to be afraid." When you ignore danger your horse does not see or hear it and no longer panics.

In such situations, small treats are useful. The chewing reflex automatically calms the horse. Pat him for

every step in the right direction during his training. Do not give up, be patient and aware that progress is dependent on the temperament of your horse.

The fun factor

Use hacking to train yourself and your horse further and improve your proficiency as a rider. Look for variations in exercise and never ride the same movement in the same place otherwise you may as well be in the school. Nature is the best riding teacher and encourages you to use all your senses and increases your awareness of the countryside. You can enjoy being at one with your horse when you ride out, but stay on permissible tracks and respect the countryside. You do however come across 'Rambos' who enjoy blocking bridleways and prevent them from being used safely by riders.

Bring variety into you and your horse's life. Go out for a day with friends for a picnic. (Remember not to ride for long distances in a dressage saddle.) And alternate between schooling and easy days where you can just enjoy your horse and you can wander among the trees. Have fun!

☞ **Tip**

Let a self confident, calm rider train your horse to cope with difficult situations. Find yourself a quiet safe horse to build you own confidence.

Riding in frost and snow

6

Sometimes it is just good for the soul to ride bareback in walk in the snow on a sunny day. However it would be safer to be wearing a proper riding hat that meets current safety standards.

Sometimes when bad weather is forecast, which you have to dress for, riding is not always possible. You cannot exercise a horse when it is cold, wet and stormy without the risk of him running away and pulling a muscle. Persistent rain does not promote muscle activity and the rider is tense and rides with hunched shoulders, which transfers to the horse.

The state of the ground

It is barely possible for the horse to move on ground that is frozen rock-hard. He cannot swing his back, step under or take weight on his haunches. On frozen or snow-covered ground the horse requires all his concentration to keep his balance and not slip. He can only work well on good ground. It is like running on tarmac without any shoes or studs to give the slightest grip.

There are some forms of weather that you can ride in without problems as long as you have access to a field, but that are not suitable for gymnastic training. The field should be flat and evenly covered with long grass

You can do in-hand work with an unshod horse in the snow provided it is not too packed down.

In-hand work

(about 20 centimetres in length) and without holes or molehills. The long frozen grass makes the ground softer and the horse can step under well. The ground cannot be used if it is frozen solid so do not trample on it if it is like this.

You can use some weather conditions to train your horse to go sideways in-hand. The aids are the same as when you are riding except that the whip becomes your inside leg. The outside rein comes over the crest of the neck to give the horse a soft contact to work into whether working forward,

It always a good exercise to teach your horse in-hand to step under and sideways from the inside leg - commonly seen when working Iberian horses.

sideways or backward. Make sure that the horse is flexed to the inside without leaning in or out. In the beginning make sure that you have full control over the outside rein so that the inside is left quiet to allow the horse to step under, his shoulder to move and so that you can keep his neck in line with his shoulders. The better the horse understands, the easier it is. Earlier I mentioned doing this with a spur in your hand. Try flexing him with both hands using a fence as a barrier.

The same goes for transitions. You can take both reins in one hand with the outside rein over the neck so you can use the whip with your inside hand. To stop the horse position your-self in front of his nose. To ask him to go forward, touch him on the side where your leg would be or just above. Walk-trot, trot-walk, walk-halt, walk-halt- rein-back-trot, transitions work very well to increase the flexibility of the horse. Remember that you can direct and control the horse with your body language when you are working him. Bending him in the Iberian fashion in snow is useful in-hand work. Hold the flexion of the neck with the inside rein and ask him to step forward from the aids, with your whip by the girth acting as the inside leg. The horse should step far under and keep his forehand almost on the spot. The outside rein again acts as a support.

The basic rules for hacking out

7

It has been a long time since horses and riders were allowed to go wherever it took their fancy. Thanks however to the work of national riding associations, in most countries a bridleway network now exists where open land is not available. Most riders know the tracks, fields and common land on which it is permissible to ride in their locality. However if you are new to an area, a few enquiries of local riding establishments and tack suppliers will soon put you in the picture.

In the UK the work of the British Horse Society has secured a comprehensive network of bridleways across the country. Most of these are shown on local Ordnance Survey maps or contact the British Horse Society at the address given below for more information. There are also local private riding clubs that work to gain access to large local land estates and farms where riders may go for an annual fee. Once again, your local riding establishments will be familiar with any such in your area.

If you do have to use the roads to gain access to off-road riding, the most important consideration is your safety. If you are not absolutely certain that your horse is as traffic proof as it is ever possible to be, always ride out with another rider. Riding hats that meet the national safety standard are essential and some form of hi-visibility clothing is also advisable. Be sure that you are wearing appropriate footwear and, if the weather permits, protect your arms against cuts and scratches from passing trees. Familiarise yourself with the Highway Code or similar local road use regulations.

Do not attempt to ride any schooling exercises on busy roads, even if they appear clear at that particular moment. Use quiet country lanes or pathways with maximum visibility in both directions.

The British Horse Society
Stoneleigh Deer Park
Kenilworth, Warwickshire. CV8 2XZ
Tel. 08701 202244
Fax 01926 707800

Credits

I would like to thank everyone who has helped with this book and for everyone who gave their time as models. I would like to thank my riding instructor Regina Johannsen not only for the photos but for riding my horses Mail (Fjord) and Valeroso(Andalusian) and especially for enthusiastically and competently training each of my horses for years which both they and I have enjoyed.

Thanks also go to Svea Lunburg and Furioso mare Second Fire, Frauke Bulow and Trakehner mare Alexa, Sandra Reinhardt and part-Quarter horse Mix, Manuela Wagenau and part-Lewitzer mare Appanachi. With their Icelandic ponies; Claudia Schmoldt and Dilkja, Elisabeth Karnath and Fendris, Beate Wise and Nasi, Manuela Kleinert-Sohn und Stelpha, Lisa Schmoldt and Boris and Bettina Schmidt, Mali's rider.

I wish you great pleasure and fun hacking with a well trained horse for many years to come